God bless you!
Gamal Alexander

Grace [2.1]

You Can Always Come Back for More

By

GAMAL T. ALEXANDER

Watersprings
PUBLISHING

GRACE 2.1
Published by Watersprings Publishing, a division of
Watersprings Media House, LLC.
P.O. Box 1284
Olive Branch, MS 38654

Unless otherwise indicated all scripture quotation is from the King James Version.

Printed in the United States of America.

Library of Congress Control Number: 2019936442

ISBN: 978-1-948877-17-6

Table of Contents

Dedication

For me, writing a book and learning to swim have much in common. For starters, I imagined both to be easier than they were, only to get started and realize that I had jumped into an entire world that had the potential to drown me! Without good coaches to guide me, and friends and family who encouraged me along the way, I would still be standing at the edge of the pool dipping my toe in the water. Complaining about how cold it is. and afraid to even get in…

So this is me saying "Thank you" to those who were patient with me, affirmed me, coached me and prayed for me. To the "Freedom Riders" who refused to let me be bound by the fear of failure, I couldn't had done this without you. To my daughters who inspire me daily, Daddy did this for the same reason he does everything else - for you. To my family who is my biggest cheering section, know that I honor you. To friends who are like family, I appreciate you.

And to my mother, to whom I never said this enough - I love you.

Thank you Compton Community, for helping me miss home a little less., and to Amber City, for the many opportunities to see love in action. Thank you, reader, for agreeing to take this journey with me, and to God, for always reminding me of Your amazing grace!

Introduction

Bills bother me, and I genuinely dislike the idea that someone is entitled to a portion of my money before it even hits my bank account. Before I see it, it's gone! Since bills bother me so much, you would think that I'd be living off the grid somewhere so I wouldn't have to be bothered. But no, I'm here in my apartment complex enjoying the amenities, driving my car, going to the gym, using my cell phone, watching Netflix. Paying the bills that never seem to go away! No matter how much I budget, save, or how many Dave Ramsey books I read, there they are-in my mailbox, inbox, or on my voicemail. Constantly in my way and on my last nerve, to the point where I'm beginning to think that I'll never get away. My entire life seems destined to pay one bill after another.

Sallie Mae has especially taught me to despise being in debt. Now SHE is a pesky princess. She just won't leave me alone! Thousands of dollars into our relationship she's still as demanding as ever. I try to break up with her, but she keeps coming back - with interest.

There is one debt, however, for which I am grateful. My favorite hymn puts it this way "Oh to grace how great a debtor, daily I'm constrained to be". And to be honest, as much as I don't like debt, I have no problem creating it. I wake up every day and start racking up more bills, accruing more debt.

Another sin for God to forgive. Another mistake for God to erase. With all the sin I've built up, you'd think grace would have run out by now. But that's what makes grace marvelous! That's why we call grace "amazing"! There's so much sin to cover and yet, His grace is sufficient. There are so many mistakes to forgive and yet, His grace is enough. As a matter of fact, it's more than enough! You may think you've used it all, but you haven't. You may think that your relationship with God is beyond repair, it isn't. You may think you've made God angry enough not to love you... you can't. No matter what you've done, where you've been or where you are right now, His grace will never run out. There will always be enough. You can always come back for more.

Day 1

Pass It On

"Each of you should use whatever gift you have received to serve others, as faithful stewards of God's grace in its various forms." 1 Peter 4:10 NIV

We often think of ourselves as receiving grace, and rightfully so. Every one of God's children has been on the receiving end of God's favor, and time and time again God has demonstrated His mercy toward us. We've received chance after chance and opportunity after opportunity. God's mercies are described as being "new every morning", and I for one am thankful that they are. I'm grateful that His mercies are new every morning because I seem to use up the complete supply every day! We are recipients of His grace and we should be grateful.

We are recipients of God's grace and we should never forget it, but how often do we forget that we have been gifted with grace that we did not deserve! If we remembered, I believe our lives would be different. We would be more understanding, compassionate, and patient. If we could simply remember that we have received this gift of grace that we do not deserve, it would change the way we interact with others, and it would change the way we live our lives.

We are recipients of God's grace and should always be grateful for it. How often do we take God's grace for granted, never pausing to even say "Thank you Lord, for all you've done for me"? Grace has become so common, and the supply is so inexhaustible that we just assume that it's always going to be there, because it's supposed to be there. God is supposed to give me grace because He's a loving God and that's His job! But we miss the part where we are undeserving.

I have held a variety of jobs since I first started working in high school. I've done everything from fast food to retail, and a host of other jobs in between. Some of the jobs have been challenging, boring, and difficult to secure. While in other cases, the employer hired me on the spot, the job included a decent salary and benefits, or I was paid in cash at the end of the day (don't ask). The common thread among all the jobs I've held is that I got paid. Whether it was a little or enough, cash or direct deposit, weekly, bi-weekly or monthly, I was compensated for my time and services. To be clear, the only reason I worked was to get paid and everything else came as a byproduct. The experience was nice and I met great people along the way, but I got paid. I also made good memories and have some pretty entertaining stories to tell (like the time I worked in a grocery store cleaning fish…remind me to tell you about that one someday). Regardless of the benefit or byproduct, the most important thing is that I got paid-and I deserved it! I put in the hours, did an honest day's work, and expected to be rewarded accordingly.

This may be difficult to understand and challenging to accept, but grace doesn't work that way. It never has, and it never will. Grace isn't a wage, a result of workin hard, or the byproduct of belonging to the right group. We are recipients of grace simply because the God we serve is gracious and He sees fit to give it to us. He just gives it to us because He wants to, and He can.

Here's a thought, since God extends His grace to us, shouldn't we extend His grace to others? It's interesting how God gives us grace freely, and yet we extend grace begrudgingly. It is as if we have managed to find the grace supply and are handing it out sparingly so that that there will be enough for us. But the grace that finds you never runs out and the grace we receive can be given over and over again. We don't have to be stingy, nor do we have to withhold. We can simply receive it and pass it on.

"It only takes a spark, to get a fire going.

And soon all those around can warm up to its glowing.

That's how it is with God's love. Once you've experienced it.

You spread His love to everyone.

You want to pass it on."

PERSONAL REFLECTION

What three examples of God's grace in your life are you grateful for?

_____

_____

_____

_____

Name someone in your life who could use a display of God's grace.

_____

_____

_____

_____

How will you react if your efforts to display God's grace are not appreciated?

_____

_____

_____

_____

Who am I praying for?

_____

_____

_____

_____

What am I praying about?

_____

_____

_____

_____

PRAYER STARTER

Gracious Father, thank You for all the grace You give to me. Help me to be just as generous in passing Your grace along to someone else. Help me today…

_____

_____

_____

_____

_____

_____

_____

_____

_____

_____

_____

_____

_____

_____

_____

_____

_____

_____

_____

_____

_____

– Amen

Day 2

The Best Gift Ever

"The last enemy to be destroyed is death..."
1 Corinthians 15:26

May I ask you a question? When did holidays become so expensive? Now don't misunderstand me because I enjoy my holidays as much as anyone else. I think we all enjoy having time to spend with family and friends, and having the opportunity to sit back and think about the things that are more important to us. Holidays can be a time for catching up and making memories, reconciling relationships, and renewing friendships. Holidays can in fact be enjoyable, but they can also be expensive.

A quick look at my calendar and my bank account winces in pain. After celebrating the New Year I have to treat my daughters for Valentine's day. Eve's birthday isn't far behind in March, followed by the Easter season. One new Easter outfit later, and we're celebrating Independence Day, then shopping on Labor Day before Terri's birthday in October. The fun really begins as Thanksgiving and Christmas roll around, but the worst part about all of this celebrating is that the culture has created the expectation that everyone has to give a gift. Valentine's day? Gift. Birthday? Gift. Christmas? Start saving now, because you have to buy a gift. Throw in a few made-up holidays (Sweetest day?), and you can understand why it can be difficult to keep up. Personally, I am running out of gift ideas.

Gift giving seems to be more difficult these days. because everyone already has everything! Ask your children what they want for their birthday, and chances are they got it last week on

Amazon. There is a store to suit every style, and if you can't find it in a store, you can have it delivered directly to your home, in your color and your size. Whatever you want, whenever you want it. Yet God managed to give us a gift that we don't already have. God has managed to give us a gift that we don't already have, fits any holiday, and we couldn't possibly pay for it. But a gift we all desperately need[ed].

Anyone who has experienced death can agree on the value of life. No amount of money can replace your loved ones being here with you. No matter how many things you enjoy, trips you take, cars you drive, or possessions you own, we would all gladly give it away to see our loved ones again. As a matter of fact, the holidays that I mentioned don't feel the same and the things we enjoy lose a little bit of their luster because the ones we lost are not here. Those who have lost someone they love will agree that if they could have just one gift, it would be to have their loved one with them again. No pictures can replace them, and no memory can substitute for them because they are gone but not forgotten. And the only gift that really matters would be to see them once again.

Death is the ultimate spoiler, and it is an appointment we may be able to postpone but can never escape. Death does not discriminate or play favorites. Neither does it take orders, bribes, or follow directions. We all have to deal with the harsh reality, but in the light of that harsh reality, we are all offered an amazing gift.

Unlike our culture, God doesn't give us this gift out of His sense of obligation or our sense of entitlement. God is love and gives us this gift as an ultimate expression of His grace. Knowing the nature of death, God gives us the ultimate gift, which is the gift of life. Eternal life. God offers us the gift of never being separated from our loved ones again or having to say goodbye. God offers us the gift of never having to plan for a funeral or having to suffer through another loss. God gives us this amazing gift. The best gift ever.

As much as I complain about giving gifts, I must confess that I love receiving them. One day I received a frame with pictures of my daughters for Father's Day. It was not the most expensive gift, but it was one of the most thoughtful gifts I have ever received. It hangs on my wall to this day. You see, it's not the expense, but the thoughtfulness behind the gift that matters most to me. For someone to take the time to observe what I like, take note of what I may or may not need, and then plan to give me a gift shows me that the person really cares. I have been known to cherish a thoughtful gift forever, because it says a lot about how much the person cares about me.

God gives the gift of life because He sees your pain. The tears you have cried over your loss have not gone unnoticed by God, and the heartbreak over your loved one has not gone unseen by God. God sees, God cares, and God has a special gift just for you. It is the gift of a world without sickness, pain or death. It is the best gift ever.

PERSONAL REFLECTION

What's the most thoughtful gift you've ever received? What was the occasion? How did it make you feel?

_____

_____

_____

_____

Why do you think the Bible calls death an "enemy"? How has this "enemy" impacted your life?

_____

_____

_____

_____

What is the first thing you will say to your loved one you lost when you see them again in heaven?

_____

_____

_____

_____

Who am I praying for?

_____

_____

_____

What am I praying about?

_____

_____

_____

_____

PRAYER STARTER
Gracious Father, I look forward to the day when death will be defeated, and I thank You for Your promise of eternal life. Help me today…

_____

_____

_____

_____

_____

_____

_____

_____

_____

_____

_____

_____

_____

_____

_____

_____

_____

_____

_____

_____

_____

_____

_____

– Amen

Day 3

For Tomorrow

*"In all thy ways acknowledge Him,
and He shall direct thy paths." Proverbs 3:6*

Said the robin to the sparrow
"I should really like to know
Why these anxious human beings
Rush about and worry so."
Said the sparrow to the robin
"Friend I think that it must be
That they have no Heavenly Father
Such as cares for you and me."
– Elizabeth Cheney

The Robin and the Sparrow might be onto something. It makes sense to live in the moment. After all, "Yesterday is history, tomorrow is a mystery. Today is the gift. That's why they call it the present". Today is really all we have because the mistakes of yesterday can't be undone, and tomorrow's trouble will come whether you and I like it or not. Today is the only point in time over which we have any control, so I get it. Live now.

Just because I'm living now doesn't mean I can't worry about later. There is something about worry that is almost irresistible. Like fast food, we are drawn to it even though it has little to no [nutritional] value at all. We can consume ourselves with worry and fret over that which we cannot change, but it doesn't make us feel any better or make us more productive. It doesn't make us smarter, more resourceful, or help us accomplish anything for that matter. Jesus put it best when He said, "Which one of you by worrying can add a single hour to your life?" (Matthew 6:27) Yet for something that accomplishes so little, worry is such a popular pastime. We do it a lot! We worry about how we will be perceived or if we be understood. We worry about being accepted. We worry about being forgiven. We worry about today, and yes, even tomorrow.

It is especially tempting to worry about things that are beyond our control. We can't change it or stop it, so we worry. It gives us something to do, but it also does something [negative] to us. As we worry, we live the trouble over and over in our minds before we ever have the opportunity to face the circumstance in reality. In that sense, tomorrow can be a thief that robs us of our peace, and takes away our comfort and energy while we deal with problems that haven't even happened yet. If we are not careful, worry about tomorrow can ruin it before it ever gets here.

And how many of us have had to deal with ruined tomorrows. A future that has been spoiled by a present that is not secure. We can't see what's coming, yet it lives with us daily. Well, God has a suggestion about how to handle tomorrow.

One day I was driving down the highway in Miami, Florida. I lived in Gainesville, Georgia at the time and was visiting Miami to spend time with friends. Not being used to driving in Florida I hopped in my car completely unprepared. I soon realized my mistake, I wasn't ready for the toll roads. You see, in my little town of Gainesville we didn't have toll booths, but here in Miami, you had to pay to drive! As I followed my friend in front of me, my anxiety began to grow. I had no change in my possession and I had no idea what happened to drivers who could not pay. All I knew was that my future was uncertain, and I was worried.

As the car ahead of me stopped to pay, I began to get my story straight. What exactly was I going to say? When my turn came, I stopped at the booth, only for her to motion me to continue driving. Thinking she had made a mistake, I rolled down my window to share my story, but there was no story needed. The car in front of me had already paid. I was worried for nothing because the trouble had already been taken care of before I ever faced it and the problem had been solved before I ever saw it. The obstacle had not been removed because the toll booth was still there, and nothing was going to change that. It was not going to just disappear. I was going to have to go through it whether I liked it or not. I would have to go through it whether I liked it or not, whether I was ready or not. I had to tough this one out because there was no other way, and the toll booth would not be removed. But by the time I got there, the issue had been resolved and all I had to do was continue on the journey.

That's how God wants us to deal with tomorrow. We spend so much time worrying about the problems up ahead that we don't ever stop to notice that the car in front of us has already paved the way! The price for your happiness has already been paid, and the way for your victory has already been made. The battles you were nervous about fighting have already been waged - and won. Your responsibility is neither to worry nor to fight, but to trust. Follow God and you will find repeatedly that once you've reached the problem, His grace has already supplied all your needs.

Don't worry about tomorrow. Just keep driving and grace will take care of the rest.

PERSONAL REFLECTION:
List three things that worry you about your future.

_____

_____

_____

_____

Do you believe it is possible to worry and pray at the same time?
If so, why? If not, why not?

_____

_____

_____

_____

Write a one sentence prayer to God about the worries you listed
above. End your prayer by thanking God in advance as you turn
over your concerns to Him today.

_____

_____

_____

Who am I praying for?

_____

_____

_____

What am I praying about?

_____

_____

_____

PRAYER STARTER

Gracious Father, Thank You for being the God of yesterday, today and tomorrow. Help me today...

_____

_____

_____

_____

_____

_____

_____

_____

_____

_____

_____

_____

_____

_____

_____

_____

_____

_____

_____

_____

_____

_____

_____

_____

_____

_____

– Amen

Day 4

All Sizes

"But He giveth more grace. Wherefore he saith, God resisteth the proud, but giveth grace unto the humble."
James 4:6

"I wonder if they have my size…"

One of the most annoying things about buying shoes is attempting to find them in my size. I'm a size 11 (just in case you ever came across a pair that you want to send my way), which just happens to be annoyingly common. It also happens to be the first size to go. Time after time I've seen the perfect pair of sneakers, or an exquisite pair of wingtips on sale. Excited, I take the display to the attendant hoping for a miracle. They disappear into the back leaving me to anticipate the good news, and then it happens - the letdown. The shoe is on sale, and it's just what I wanted, but they don't have my size.

Honestly, I used to be more enthusiastic about buying shoes. I used to search for sales and browse the websites looking for deals, but the size thing discouraged me. If my feet were just a bit smaller or larger, shoes would be more available for me. As it stands, if I don't get there in time, I'm out of luck. They never have my size.

I thought I was the only one with this problem until I started working in a shoe store years ago. I discovered that sizing is an issue that's much more common than we realize. It seems as if everyone is trying to find the right fit. Some feet are narrow. Some feet are wide. Some feet are unusually small. Some feet are unusually large. There are those who have to put in a great deal of time and effort just trying to find a shoe that fits them, and they can't simply ignore the task. You see, if you are going to spend any significant time in a shoe, the shoe needs to fit. Gone are the days when a person can make exceptions for shoes that are cute but uncomfortable. The shoe may look incredible on your feet and match perfectly with your outfit, but the most important factor to be considered before you decide to take it home should be, "Does this actually fit?" and "Do they have this in my size?"

We all wear different sizes because we are all different people. We have different backgrounds, cultures, talents and abilities, flaws, and needs. That's why, when it comes to grace, we may advertise that "one size fits all", but truthfully, that approach doesn't really work. Our need for grace is universal, and we all need to be given favor from God that is completely undeserved. Everyone needs the forgiveness, compassion, and kindness of a Savior. And everyone needs to experience the limitless love of our Heavenly Father. We all need rescuing. We all need rescuing and restoring and at some point, everyone's faith will need reviving. So, although the need is definitely universal, our needs come in different sizes.

Some of our needs come in "small". So small in fact, that these are the needs for which we often neglect to pray, choosing instead to handle the issues ourselves. These are the questions we already have answered, the battles we easily win, the goals we achieve ahead of schedule. It doesn't seem right to bother God with the small stuff. Why? We've got it under control. We have what I need, know where we're going, and already have things figured out. Yet grace comes in small, because we need grace for the small stuff too. There is no area of our lives too small to be ignored by God. He cares about our tiny problems because we are His children, and He wants His favor to cover every aspect of our lives. If you need grace for an area in your life that seems small, then ask. Grace comes in your size.

Many of our needs are "medium," and these are the most difficult to handle. Everyone has them! They are nothing special, they don't keep us from walking with God, and they don't ruin our experience. They're just normal, everyday problems about which everybody complains. Your teenager talks back? Great! Join the club. Hate your job? So, does everybody else! Having money problems? Who isn't having money problems? When you find the place where they are handing out perfect, problem-free, lives please let me know- I'll be on the first flight over. The reality is that everyone's going through something, which makes it difficult to ask for grace. We are tempted to settle because everybody settles. We are tempted to stay where we are because everybody's there. Everyone's marriage goes through challenging times, and everyone gets sick occasionally. Troubles seems to most often come in medium because it's a popular size, and everyone seems to be wearing it. But grace comes in medium too.

Grace also comes in "large." The challenges that are so big, that we are afraid to ask about because we are sure the answer will be no. The problems that overwhelm us, the pain that makes us numb, trials that seem to come in wave after wave and heartache that never ends. Some of our needs are large. Large enough to shake our faith. Large enough to drive a wedge between us and God. Large enough to keep us up at night and to make us wonder if we have a God that really, truly cares. Your need for grace may be large, but God's supply of grace is everlasting. Whether small, medium, or large, God has grace enough. Minimal needs, mundane challenges, or a need that is as large as a mountain, God has grace enough to cover it all.

You don't have to worry about His Grace. He has your size.

PERSONAL REFLECTION

List a "small", "medium", and "large" problem in your life that needs God's grace:

Small:_____

Medium: _____

Large:_____

Have you ever felt that a problem in your life was either too small for God to notice, or too big for God to handle? Do you have a problem that fits into either category now? Write a one sentence prayer to God submitting that problem to Him.

Consider the following list of prayer requests. What do you need from God? Circle all that apply to you:

Relationships	Health	Finances
Family	School	Finding employment
Guidance	Forgiveness	Breaking a habit

Who am I praying for?

_____

_____

_____

_____

What am I praying about?

_____

_____

_____

_____

PRAYER STARTER

Gracious Father, I thank You that whatever I need, You can supply. Help me today…

_____

_____

_____

_____

_____

_____

_____

_____

_____

_____

_____

_____

_____

_____

_____

_____

_____

_____

_____

_____

_____

_____

_____

_____

_____

– Amen

Day 5

You Can

*"For God so loved the world, that He gave
His only begotten Son..." John 3:16*

I love stories. I love creating them, telling them and experiencing them. I believe in the power of stories and admire the people who have dedicated their lives to ensuring that the best stories continue to be told for years to come. There were so many reasons for me to fall in love with stories. For starters, I believe stories to be the most effective form of communication human beings have ever known, and our values are best communicated through story. Our history was preserved through story and our culture lives on through story. Stories remind us of who we are, and light the way as we journey towards who we strive to be. I also fell in love with stories largely because stories open doors. Not only do stories deal with the present, but they can build windows into the future as well. Stories can allow the hearer to stand in the here and now and glance into the "not yet", looking forward to things yet unseen. Stories give the imagination the tools to build a world where anything is possible. Stories blow the doors off limits and shatter the shackles of our boundaries. In short, when our circumstances try to convince us that we can't, we have always been able to tell stories that remind us that we can.

Stories are important because reality is difficult. If we are not careful, we can find ourselves locked in a prison of our own lack of possibility, serving life sentences with no possibility of parole. Grace can become a fantasy and new beginnings a mere afterthought as dreams are replaced by the drudgery of the day to day. If we are not careful the lack of a story can cause some to stop dreaming, and the lack of a dream can cause some to surrender. Maybe this is the way life is supposed to be.

I don't believe we can survive without our stories. Walt Disney proved as much by using his stories to make our lives better. As Disney told stories, we learned from him, we dreamed with him, we followed him, and we felt with him. Disney created a world in which anything was possible, where the everyday person could escape from the drudgery that they encountered daily. We needed those stories.

Stan Lee also told stories of loyalty, family, victory and valor. By doing so, he proved that we needed a place to go when life threatened to get unbearable, difficult, and cold. His were stories of courage, strength and the human ideal. His were characters who conquered their fatal flaws and rose to be the best versions of themselves. Stan Lee told stories of loyalty and family. He told stories of victory and valor. Stan Lee spent his life telling stories that will be told and retold long after he is gone. We needed those stories too.

Here's a story that I believe we cannot live without and I don't think we hear enough of. It is the story of Jesus. It's the story that has been misrepresented and misunderstood, yet must be told. It is a story of tragedy, triumph, abandonment, and promise. It is also a story of family and loyalty, and that only covers the first few years of Jesus' life! We need this story too! We need the story of Jesus.

We need the story of the promised Deliverer who was born to a poor teenage girl in Bethlehem. We need the story of the fugitive family who migrated to Egypt to save the life of the Savior of all humankind. We need the story of the carpenter's Son who kept company with fishermen and counted tax collectors as His followers and friends. The story of the Redeemer who lived, died, and rose again from the grave. We need this story! Why? Because this story will open up possibilities and help believe that anything is indeed possible. This story will take the limits off our lives so that while others say we can't, we can confidently remember the story and declare that we definitely can.

We can be healthy, happy and whole. We can depend on God to keep His promises and wait on deliverance to come. In a world that says we can't, the story of Jesus says that we can, because God did. God did not hold back. He sent His Son to live on earth and then die for our sins, only to be risen again. As Jesus walked this earth, the eyes of the blind were opened, the lame were able to walk again, and even the dead were raised. What a story! We need the story of Jesus and His grace because it says at its core, that God can and God did. Most importantly, the story of Jesus tells us that if God can, and He empowers you, then you can too.

PERSONAL REFLECTION

What are some of the ways our world would be different without the story of Jesus?

_____

_____

_____

_____

If you had to explain what Jesus meant to you in one sentence of 10 words or less, what would you say?

_____

_____

_____

_____

Read John 3:16 again. Now list the most important word in the sentence and explain your choice.

_____

_____

_____

_____

What am I praying about?

_____

_____

_____

Who am I praying for?

_____

_____

_____

PRAYER STARTER

Gracious Father, I thank You for the story of Jesus and the impact it has made in my life. Please give me an opportunity today to share that story with someone else. Help me today...

–Amen

Day 6

Baggage Check

"Therefore they inquired of the Lord further, if the man should yet come thither. And the Lord answered, Behold, he hath hid himself among the stuff."
1 Samuel 10:22

The most historic day in Israel's history had finally arrived, and they were finally ready to crown a new king. The road to this point had been unconventional to say the least, yet God like any earthly father, had decided that He couldn't say "no" all the time. This time He would go against His original intentions and expand the parameters of His plan (as is His prerogative). "They have not rejected you". You could hear the noticeable pain in the voice of the Almighty. Yet Israel's rightful king would abdicate His throne. He would step aside for one, who while chosen to be a successor, would never be big enough, strong enough, or wise enough to fill those shoes. God would once again be merciful and give His children what they wanted. God would allow Israel to have a king.

God had chosen their king and He had chosen well. It was a logical choice, with loads of potential. The king God chose looked the part and was the tallest man in the entire kingdom, standing head and shoulders above everyone else. He was handsome and had the bearings of a leader. God had not chosen Saul for spite, but had chosen him to succeed! This would be a king they could be proud of, a leader that would inspire confidence, a leader they could follow. With Samuel advising him, and God by his side,

Saul's reign was set to be a resounding success.

What an incredible honor to be chosen by God! It's an honor not to be taken lightly, and an honor that all of God's children enjoy. We are a "chosen generation". Each one of us is called by God for service, and selected by God for greatness. This means that our lives are not random reactions to the events that come our way. We are much more than that. We are called! God has planned our lives intentionally. God has planned our lives intentionally, and has given us every opportunity to succeed in partnership with Him. We are not afterthoughts, nor is any one of us a mistake. We are neither forgotten nor are we failures. We may have failed at something, but we have been called. We may have had setbacks, be we have been called. Life for you might be far less than ideal, but you have been chosen. You have been called, God was intentional and He has a purpose and a plan for you.

God was intentional, and He meant to do what He did. He called Saul, and now the day had come for his reign to finally begin. The coronation of Israel's first king would see pomp and circumstance like never before. His would be a coronation fit for a monarch, and a celebration to go down in history. All the preparations were set, the people in place and the dignitaries were gathered. The ceremony was set to begin, but as the officials reviewed the checklist, they noticed that they were missing something. Was it the crown? No, they had that. Was it the robe? No, they had that too. Was it the throne? That was in place. They looked around and thought, until it finally hit them. They had everything they needed for a coronation, except a king.

Saul had gone into hiding! Even though he had been called, he refused to show up to fulfill his destiny. Can you imagine being selected to be great and yet refusing to show up and participate in your own greatness? That was Saul's struggle and at times we struggle here too. Chosen to be great, we refuse to show up and participate in our own greatness. God can't possibly be serious, after all. Me? Launch my own business or own my own home? Me? Debt free, employing otheers or climbing the ladder of success? Me? Being an inspiration and a testimony of God's amazing grace? I don't think so. Like Saul, we have all been chosen, and like Saul, many run and hide, refusing to participate in their own success.

So, where did Saul hide? The Lord found him hiding "behind his baggage". Apparently, Saul had not received the memo that he was going to be crowned king! As far as I know, Saul had never been king before, so none of the supplies from his previous life could have possibly fit his new one. Even if they were similar, his being king would have earned him an upgrade! Anything from his future would have automatically been better than his past, yet he refused to leave his past behind. Instead he carried his "baggage" with him and used it to hide.

God wants to do so much for us, but He can only do it if we allow Him. It's up to us to let go of our baggage and walk in God's grace. The past can stay right where it is, in the past! His grace has allowed me to leave it behind and embrace a future that is brighter than I could have ever dreamed. God has chosen me, and I choose to show up for my success! My best is yet to come.

PERSONAL REFLECTION

What bothers you the most about your past?

a) Mistakes

b) Missed opportunities

c) Mistreatment

d) Other

e) All of the above

What relationship should we have with the past?

_____

_____

_____

_____

How does the past harm us? How can it be used for our benefit?

_____

_____

_____

_____

What am I praying about?

_____

_____

_____

_____

Who am I praying for?

_____

_____

_____

_____

PRAYER STARTER

Gracious Father, I praise You for setting me free from the mistakes of my past. I thank You for the lessons learned and I ask Your forgiveness for the places where I strayed from Your will. Help me today...

_____

_____

_____

_____

_____

_____

_____

_____

_____

_____

_____

_____

_____

_____

_____

_____

_____

_____

_____

_____

_____

_____

_____

_____

– Amen

Day 7

Covered

*"And the Lord made for Adam and his wife
garments of skins and clothed them..."
Genesis 3:21*

Clothing is everywhere! Have you noticed? There are literally hundreds of brands, styles, and colors to choose from, that range from affordable to, "You paid WHAT for a pair of jeans?". No matter who you are, you can't escape dealing with clothes. Buying them, wearing them, cleaning them, has all, at some point, been a part of your life. And if you were like me in high school, clothing WAS your life.

It seems crazy as I look back on it now, but as a 14-year-old kid growing up in Raleigh, North Carolina, what I wore meant everything to me. I had just moved from Tampa, Florida and was all set to start at a new high school. That year, everything changed. I went from a relatively small school, to the largest one I had ever seen. I went from a private school to a public school for the first time ever. I stood out and I knew it. And then there were my clothes...

Let's just say my parents didn't have the best fashion sense, especially when it came to a teenage boy. "A hundred dollars for a pair of sneakers?" My Jamaican mother would ask? "I don't care who Michael Jordan is! The answer is no!" Often, I went to school looking more like the children we sponsored at Christmas time than the rest of the teenagers walking around the cafe. "For the price of a cup of coffee, you can buy this teen some decent clothes…" Needless to say, I hated just about everything I wore!

While we all wear different types of clothing, (and let's face it, some of our choices are more "interesting" than others) at the very least, we wear clothing because most of us can't afford to walk around naked. Clothing helps us to express ourselves and can serve as a status symbol. But even more than that, clothing covers. You don't see all of my faults because I hide them beneath my clothes. My body isn't perfect. There are scars, blemishes and extra "luggage" in places where extra "luggage" shouldn't be. I'd like to think that I'm comfortable in my own skin, but I don't want everyone seeing everything! Think about it. Even the skimpiest of outfits will attempt to keep private parts private. No one wants everyone seeing everything!

And yet when it comes to us, that's exactly what God sees. Everything. Whether your outfit is tailored or not, skimpy or not, expensive or not, God sees everything. There's nothing that escapes His glance and nothing that's outside of His gaze. He sees the stuff I wish wasn't there, and sees the places where I would rather He never look. When it comes to God, there's no use pretending, no sense in hiding, and no point in lying. God sees it all. It's as if I'm naked.

There's a vulnerability to being naked in front of someone else. That's one of the reasons I don't like going to the doctor. Undressing should be done in private, not in preparation for an exam. After all, I don't want anyone to see me! Sure, they can see me, with my clothes on, that way I can give them the look I want them to see and I can show them what I don't mind them viewing. But I repeat, I don't want anyone to, you know… "see" me. No one. Especially not God. That's as vulnerable as I could ever possibly be, and an exam for which I'll never be ready. Yet God sees me anyway, and He sees you too.

And I believe He's telling us, it's ok.

When God first saw Adam and Eve naked, He acted. He did

for them what He does for you and me. He made a covering. It seems simple, but I'm going to invite you to look at that again. He killed an animal and made a garment out of the skins. God didn't just purchase something suitable, He made a sacrifice in order to cover their shame, because that's what being covered is all about.

The enemy would like nothing more than to leave you exposed in the naked shame of your past. Every flaw laid bare., every misstep opened up for judgment, and every sin highlighted for the universe to see. His plan was for your nakedness to be your eternal identity. He wanted your sin to be how you see yourself and God saw you, forever. But thank God for covering! I can bring my nakedness to God and know that the blood of Jesus covers those imperfections. Now that I'm covered by Jesus' blood, grace allows me to walk around as if I've never sinned. The covering took a sacrifice for which I am grateful, and Christ's righteousness is a garment I'll gladly wear.

I have more than my fair share of flaws, and God knows about them. He has seen me naked! He still loves me! And His grace has covered me.

PERSONAL REFLECTION

Are you comfortable with God knowing everything about you? Why or Why not?

_____

_____

_____

_____

If you were given a choice, is there anything about you that you would rather God not see?

_____

_____

_____

_____

What sacrifice did God make to cover your sins? What does that sacrifice mean to you?

_____

_____

_____

_____

What am I praying about today?

_____

_____

_____

_____

Who am I praying for today?

_____

_____

_____

_____

PRAYER STARTER

Gracious Father, thank You for the blood of Jesus shed on Calvary that covers me! I have no need to ever be embarrassed about my life, because You know me inside and out and You still love me. Help me today…

_____

_____

_____

_____

_____

_____

_____

_____

_____

_____

_____

_____

_____

_____

_____

_____

_____

_____

_____

_____

_____

_____

_____

– Amen

Day 8

There Is Enough

"My grace is enough for you…" 2 Corinthians 12:9
(New Century Version)

I've always found a certain security in having enough, and I like that feeling. I like the feeling of knowing that I'm prepared, knowing that needs are provided for, and emergencies will be covered. I like knowing that things are taken care of and that I don't have to worry. Chances are, you do too.

Let's face it: not having enough can be embarrassing. Like the time I offered to pay for dinner for myself and a friend at a restaurant only to be met with a request to "try another method of payment." How embarrassing! And then there was the time I decided to go car shopping for the upgrade I desperately needed (and thought I completely deserved). "Not enough credit" they said… How about the check I wrote in college to cover a late-night trip to IHOP. (I was in college and hungry, you already know where this is going…) Insufficient funds AND an overdraft fee! And the pancakes weren't even that good! And I'll never forget the road trip from Maryland to New York that left me stranded on the Delaware Memorial bridge because I ran out of gas. To add insult to injury, I could see the gas station less than a mile away! I could see it, I just couldn't reach it. With all the good intentions in the world, I had run out. I just didn't have enough… and everyone driving past me on the highway that evening pointed and gestured because they knew it.

Not having enough can be tough to hide, and it can also be embarrassing. Any wonder why the hosts of the wedding at Cana went into such a panic? They were the ones throwing the party. They were the ones responsible for the refreshments. They were the ones that, by default, promised a good time. It was their responsibility to make sure that all the guests had eaten and enjoyed, and yet, at a critical juncture in the festivities, they ran out of wine. They didn't have enough. How embarrassing! Most of us know what that feels like, and we avoid that feeling at all costs.

Not only do we avoid that feeling, but we try not to contribute to it either. When it's discovered that someone doesn't have enough, we do the polite thing and let the matter go. After all, the insufficiency in and of itself is shameful. No need to add to "their lacking" with an extra "look at them". Better to quietly allow them to replenish than continue to drain the valuable resources they already don't have. We all know that people require a lot, and we all know how demanding we can be. So, we try to pitch in and not make it worse.

I've been ashamed of my limited resources, and I've also been ashamed of my astronomical need. Especially when it comes to Jesus. I need so much! There's always a mistake to be forgiven or some brokenness to be restored. There's always more demand for grace than there is supply, because my life seems to demand so much. Could there ever be enough?

Jesus opens the pantry of grace and gives us a peek inside. And yes, there is enough. "His grace is sufficient for you." Despite my seemingly insatiable appetite for everything that isn't good for me, the inventory is still the same: "My grace is sufficient for you." Whatever you need. However, many times you may need it. It will always be there. Try to exhaust God's grace and there will always be more. Try to outrun God's grace and you will always be caught. Try to out maneuver God's grace and it will follow you "all the days of your life". You don't have to be ashamed of needing it, because God will never be hesitant to provide it. There will always be enough.

Thanksgiving at Mom's house was always a bit of a madhouse. Come to think of it, she liked it that way. Every year the house would be full of people, some of whom I didn't even know, but all of whom were hungry. Taught to be polite, family would let the guest eat first. You don't know fear until you've seen a swarm of people descending upon a table of food that was supposed to be yours! And yet there was never a need to panic because Mom always had an extra pan put aside, and an extra plate or two in hiding. No need to worry. There would always be enough.

God has an extra serving of grace put aside just for you. There's no need to worry and no reason to fear. There will always be more than enough.

PERSONAL REFLECTION

Today we were reminded that God has more than enough grace to cover every sin. How does that make you feel?

_____

_____

_____

God never runs out of patience with us. How should that influence our treatment of each other?

_____

_____

_____

_____

Innocent animals died so that Adam and Eve might be covered with their skins. What does that mean to you?

_____

_____

_____

_____

What am I praying about today?

_____

_____

_____

Who am I praying for today?

_____

_____

_____

PRAYER STARTER

Gracious Father, I thank You for the grace You show by covering me. I am humbled when I think about Your incredible sacrifice on the cross for my sins. I am grateful that You know me best and love me still. Help me today…

– Amen

Day 9

Over and Over Again

*"For I delivered to you as of first importance
what I also received, that Christ Jesus died
for our sins according to the Scriptures."*
1 Corinthians 15:3

Sports can be deceptive, because athletes make sports look easy. The best athletes, the truly gifted, tend to leave the spectators with a feeling that they have witnessed something magical or superhuman. Something only the most gifted among us could ever do. Go behind the scenes, however, and you will see a very different picture being painted. While the most elite athletes are blessed with rare talents and uncommon abilities, more often than not, the professional owes his expertise to hours and hours of paying attention to, and practicing the fundamentals. Countless hours have been spent dribbling and shooting the basketball and week after week has been spent perfecting the art of throwing and catching a football. They have practiced the game and honed their craft to the point where the fundamentals have become second nature. This is the mastery that gives them the success we celebrate.

You can always tell those who try to skip the fundamentals. No matter what sport it is, there are always those who rush past the basics because they can't wait to make magic happen, and instead they end up making a mess. The spirit is willing, but the game is weak, and you can only build a strong game on a foundation of strong fundamentals. Before you emulate your favorite player's highlights, you have to emulate your favorite player's habits. Hours and hours of practice. Day after day of sacrifice. You practice and practice. Over and over again.

Not only does an elite player in any sport master the fundamentals, but they never stray too far from them. As a matter of fact, everything they do, while it may look creative, is simply a variation of the fundamentals. What's more, if a player should ever see a decline in his or her effectiveness or productivity, a good coach will often return to the fundamentals. That's how every player improves. Observe a great athlete and the fundamentals are never far away.

The Christian walk can also be deceptive. Great Christians like Paul can make it look easy. We read about his exploits, and there's no denying it. When it comes to living for Jesus, the Apostle Paul is one of the best of the best. He is the quintessential Christian. The definition of what it means to follow Jesus. He witnesses without flinching and remains steadfast in his faith without wavering. You can't help but read Paul's writings, study Paul's life and think to yourself, "I want to be like him when I grow up." Paul makes it look easy, and yet for Paul the Christian walk wasn't easy at all. How do I know? He says so himself! In Romans 7:19-25 Paul outlines the struggle he has living for Jesus – and what a titanic struggle it is! The good that Paul intends to do is constantly hijacked by the evil that Paul has every intention of evicting. Sounds like a complete and total mess! Actually, it sounds very familiar.

You and I have seen this struggle before because we've seen it play out in our own lives. We have seen the battles up close and personal and we have wondered, time and time again exactly how these giants of the faith like the apostle Paul, make this walk look so easy. Is there a special kind of grace that I just don't know about? Actually, there's grace available, but there's nothing particularly special about it at all. The secret? Paul has mastered the fundamentals. He goes back to the gospel over and over again. Paul is absolutely clear that Jesus died for his sins and he knows that he is loved by God. Paul's belief system isn't very complicated at all. Even throughout the book of Romans, widely recognized as a summation of what Paul believes, Paul remains consistent. He practices the fundamentals: Jesus, grace, love, the cross, and the Gospel. Over and over again.

If you're having trouble with your Christian walk, it may be time to simplify the "game" so to speak, and return to the fundamentals. We have a habit of complicating our faith, when in fact it doesn't need to be complicated at all. As a matter of fact, in order to grow, develop and advance, we must master the basics. What's more, we will find that as we mature, the fundamentals will never be far behind.

Jesus. Grace. Love. The Cross. The Gospel. Over and over again.

PERSONAL REFLECTION

Why does Paul continue to repeat and revisit the fundamentals of the faith? Why should we?

_____

_____

_____

_____

Have you ever complicated your relationship with Jesus? How?

_____

_____

_____

_____

What is one way you can get back to the fundamentals in your relationship with God today?

_____

_____

_____

_____

What am I praying about today?

_____

_____

_____

_____

Who am I praying for today?

_____

_____

_____

_____

PRAYER STARTER

Gracious Father, I desperately needed to be saved and I thank You for sending Jesus to save me, simple as that. Help me today...

– Amen

Day 10

Looking for You

"But Noah Found Grace in the eyes of the Lord."
Genesis 6:8

Grace comes across as something that happens to the fortunate. After all, we always consider ourselves lucky when we get something for free! And for good reason: free doesn't happen every day.

I can count only a handful of times when I've ever won anything or got anything for free. I know people who win prizes all the time. You know those people. They seem to be at the right place at the right time. They always have their name called, their number always comes up and they are always announced as, "Our lucky winners". Unfortunately, that was never me. I just don't have that type of "luck", and my name never comes up. I never get the free tickets, or the free prize, or whatever it is that they happen to be giving away. I never get anything for free.

So, while I'm happy for Noah, I can't relate. The Bible says that Noah "found" grace. It was as if he was simply walking along, minding his own business, and boom! He just happened to run right into a big old stack of grace. Lucky Noah! He didn't ask for it, he wasn't planning for it, and he wasn't looking for it. He didn't deserve it, but there it was. Noah found grace.

My mother used to go through her old pocketbooks and occasionally find money. You could tell how much she found by her reaction. If she found a penny, a nickel or a dime, her reaction would be barely noticeable. If she found a quarter or a dollar, there would be more excitement and enthusiasm in her tone. One time she found a $100 bill. Completely unexpected, my mother came across $100 she had not planned for. I don't have to tell you that mom was overjoyed. We were all overjoyed! Mom found an unexpected blessing with no strings attached. Mom found grace.

But I don't ever win anything, find anything, or get anything for free. Sure, I was happy for mom, and I'm happy for anyone who is fortunate enough to discover an unexpected blessing. Whether it's a $100 bill or a free donut from Krispy Kreme, an unexpected blessing is always cause for celebration. However, while I'm happy for everyone who gets free stuff, I can't relate to you, and I couldn't relate to Noah. That is, until I read the text again.

The Bible says that Noah found grace, "In the eyes of the Lord." The eyes were what I was missing. That's what I couldn't understand, and why I couldn't relate. At first glance, it seemed as if Noah found grace the same way we all find free stuff. He was wandering around and eventually, he found it. However, I believe the Bible is saying more. God was the one who was looking. God was the one who was searching, and while He was searching, He had grace in His eyes. God was looking for people to spare from the upcoming flood He would visit upon the world, and He was looking for someone who was faithful upon whom He could show His unmerited favor. God was looking for someone to bless, someone to spoil, someone to save... and He found Noah. Noah wasn't looking for God, but God was looking for him!

And isn't that always the case? We don't go looking for God. If that was the sequence, then we would be in trouble. Human beings have always been woefully ineffective in their search for God. We don't know what to look for, where to look, or where to start. We look through the lenses of our own biases and through the frames of our own fears. We've never been successful when it comes to looking for God, so God has always had to come looking for us. In Genesis when Adam and Eve fell to the tempter and sin sent them hiding, God came looking. When Israel rebelled repeatedly and needed reminders of their Shepherd's love for them, God came looking. And when the "fullness of time had come" (Galatians 4:4) and a Savior had to be sent as a light into an abysmally darkened world, God came looking. And every time God looked, God found us with grace in His eyes.

God is still looking for us, even if we aren't looking for Him. God is looking for broken people to restore, hurting people to heal and lost people to bring back to Him. God is looking for you and me, don't be afraid, God is looking for you, and when He finds you, there will be grace in His eyes.

PERSONAL REFLECTION

Why is it important to understand that God looks for us before we look for Him?

_____

_____

_____

_____

"God is looking for people to shower with His grace." What does that mean for those who do not have a personal relationship with Jesus?

_____

_____

_____

_____

If grace is so valuable, why would God not wait for us to come to Him?

_____

_____

_____

_____

What am I praying about today?

_____

_____

_____

_____

Who am I praying for today?

_____

_____

_____

_____

PRAYER STARTER

Gracious Father, I thank You for making the first move and looking for me. Your grace and mercy pursued me even when I didn't know what was best for me. For that I am grateful. Help me today…

– Amen

Day 11

It's Working

"Therefore we do not lose heart; but indeed, if our outward man is being brought to decay yet our inner self is being renewed day by day."
2 Corinthians 4:16 NASV

My local gym goes through the same yearly routine. Chances are, yours does too. Just before the holidays the place is empty. The regulars work out, but there's plenty of room. Except for the diehards and those who occasionally drop by, there's not much action. Nothing to see here folks, until New Years. Come January 1st, the new year's resolution crowd arrives, and they come with a vengeance! Now the crowd isn't all bad. Sure, it may be a little more crowded than the regulars are used to, but there's an energy and an excitement, a new life that comes to the gym that just can't be denied. It's fun having people around!

Most of the people who join or return for the new year come for a reason. They want to see a change. They are tired of the way things are, they are tired of the way they are, and they have decided that enough is enough and it's time to do something different. They identify the problem (the problem is staring at them in the mirror) and they have decided on a solution. Begin an exercise program and then they attack the problem with all of the enthusiasm they can muster. Classes are full, exercise machines are taken and dumbbells are all over the floor. And then slowly but surely, something happens.

By about March, things return to normal. The wide-eyed exercise enthusiasts are gone, having been disappointed with their lack of results. You see, what they never tell you when you sign up for your gym membership is that for this, or any method to work, you have to keep doing it. It will get boring, and painful, and tedious, but you have to continue. The exercise is critical, but consistency is the key. Even during the times when you don't see anything, you have to keep working out and eventually the results will come.

Most things happen instantly in our culture, which makes patience a problem. Google a definition, and the computer spits out an answer immediately. Post a picture on social media, and people begin to weigh in immediately. Instant message a friend, and you can get a response immediately. It's an "instant" message after all. There's no need to wait for the result and there's definitely no need to try again. Is there any wonder why Christian growth can cause so much anxiety? Like the new year's resolution crew, many want to see the results of spiritual growth immediately. I pray; therefore, I grow. I read; therefore I know. But nothing can be farther from the truth.

The Christian life includes both the act of justification and the process of sanctification. Once we accept Jesus as our Savior, He counts us as one of His. We are credited with His sinless life and we are treated by God as if we were perfect people. That's called "justification". All is forgiven and all is immediately right with God. However, we are not perfect people. Far from it. As a matter of fact, we are not even spiritually mature people. The day after you are baptized you will more than likely make the same mistakes, and the year after you accept Jesus you still struggle with your Christian walk. The process that involves Christian growth and development is known as "Sanctification". This process is what takes an entire lifetime, and this process requires God's grace.

Day after day God molds us, shapes us, and gradually makes us more and more like Jesus. The longer you walk with the Lord, the more you will eventually notice changes in your life.

The problem is that most of these changes take time. Slowly and steadily we grow and develop until one day, we look back and we are different, and better people than what we used to be.

Growing up I was obsessed with my height. My mother was only 5' 3" and if I could help it, I was determined to be taller than her! I ate, and slept and measured myself daily, hoping to somehow make growth happen by sheer willpower. Fortunately, someone got a hold of me and taught me that growth never works that way. I had to exercise, eat, rest, and trust that things were working. Eventually I would see the changes I so desperately wanted to see. Later, I learned that this is exactly how the Christian life works. We want to grow so badly but nothing we do can force the process. God invites us to walk with Him, stay in His word, rest in His grace, and trust that He is working in our lives. In His time and by His grace, our lives will produce the changes we need to see.

PERSONAL REFLECTION

How can you be absolutely sure that Jesus is working in your life?

_____

_____

_____

_____

Give one example of an area in your life that has improved because of Jesus.

_____

_____

_____

_____

List three areas in your life where you would like to see significant improvement by this time next year? What does "significant improvement" look like to you?

_____

_____

_____

_____

What am I praying about today?

_____

_____

_____

Who am I praying for today?

_____

_____

_____

PRAYER STARTER

Gracious Father, I'm thankful that You're still working on me. While I am far from perfect, You have not given up on me yet- and You never will. Thank You. Help me today...

_____

_____

_____

_____

_____

_____

_____

_____

_____

_____

_____

_____

_____

_____

_____

_____

_____

_____

_____

_____

_____

_____

– Amen

Day 12

You're Still Mine

"For His anger endureth but a moment; in His favour is life: weeping may endure for a night, but joy cometh in the morning."
Psalm 30:5

Here's a little secret I learned about children. They're really, really cute, but they can make you really, really mad.

Ok, that may not actually be a secret at all. If you've ever raised, worked with, or even been around children for any significant length of time you "discovered" that bit of information a long time ago. Those faces are adorable, the smiles can light up a room and brighten your day, and the expressions on their faces are priceless! Those little hands and feet can bring such joy to any household. And the laughter - How can anyone not enjoy the laughter of a child! There's something about the laughter of children that makes the joy contagious. Children start laughing, and pretty soon you want to start laughing too. The feeling is beautiful!

None of that changes the fact that they can make you very, very mad.

On March 13, 2005 I was blessed with our first little angel. And what an adorable little angel she was! I stared at her for hours on end as I allowed those beautiful brown eyes to melt my heart and change my life. Like every first-time parent, my child could do no wrong. Crying? That's how babies communicate. Isn't she precious? Pooping? There's barely any smell! I could change these diapers all day! Feedings? So what if it's 3am! Babies need to eat at 3am, and God put daddies on earth to help them do just that. For about the first three weeks of her life my precious little one was a sure-fire nominee for baby sainthood. Then she began to grow. And I began to learn the cold hard truth that while babies are cute, they can make you really, really mad.

Colic is defined as a "severe, often fluctuating pain in the abdomen caused by intestinal gas or obstruction in the intestines. It is suffered especially by babies." At just about 8 weeks old, colic was suffered by my baby. Oh boy did she suffer. It broke my heart to hear my little one cry. What I wasn't prepared for was the fact that she would continue to cry, and cry, and cry. At first, I felt sympathy, then fatigue, then powerlessness, and then anger. The more she cried and the more we tried and the more we failed to comfort her, the more frustrated we became. I'm not proud of it, but our precious bundle of joy managed to get me very, very angry.

Maybe you haven't had any experience with crying babies, but God has had plenty of experience with you. Your heavenly Father thinks the world of you. He created you and sent His Only Son to die for you. His love for you is eternal, and yet you and I disappoint God. We stray from God, rebel against God, and dare I say, make Him angry.

Of course, Eve's crying was not her fault. The baby was sick! Dad had no reason to be angry you say. She didn't know. Don't worry, over the years Eve would have plenty of opportunities and plenty of practice making her old man irate. About 2.5 years later, Eve was joined by her little sister Terri, who has also proven skillfully adept at driving me up a wall! Their powers combined are the stuff of legends. Oh, how I love my little angels of destruction.

One thing I have noticed however, is that no matter what they get into, what stunt they pull, or what they say or not say, I can't stay mad at them for long. They may disappoint me at times, and there are times when the things they do or say make me sad. Other times they make me see pure red, but it's never for long. I cannot stay angry with them, because they are mine. Whatever the challenge, we have to address it. Whatever the problem, we must fix it. Whatever the disappointment, we must handle it. Why? Because despite what they may do or what I may feel, those girls are mine. Nothing in the world can ever change the fact that they belong to me.

I can go on all day about how much I love my girls, and yet I can't begin to describe your Heavenly Father's love for you. You belong to Him! There may be times when the consequences of your decisions cause you to feel forsaken and forgotten, but don't believe for a moment that your God no longer loves you. You belong to Him! You may feel disconnected and isolated but please don't despair. You belong to Him! No matter what, you are still His, He is still your Father, and no one could ever love you more.

PERSONAL REFLECTION

Is there anything you can do to make God love you more? Is there anything you can do to make God love you less? Explain your answer.

_____

_____

_____

Describe one instance in which God demonstrated His limitless love for you? How did you express your gratitude?

_____

_____

_____

_____

What does "belonging" to God mean to you? How does this belonging affect your life?

_____

_____

_____

_____

What am I praying about today?

_____

_____

_____

Who am I praying for today?

_____

_____

_____

PRAYER STARTER

Gracious Father, there is nothing I can do to make you love me more or love me less. I belong to you! For that, Oh God, I am thankful. Help me today...

_____

_____

_____

_____

_____

_____

_____

_____

_____

_____

_____

_____

_____

_____

_____

_____

_____

_____

_____

_____

_____

_____

_____

_____

– Amen

Day 13

The Same

"And forgive us our debts, as we forgive our debtors."
Matthew 6:12

"It's not fair!"

I can't begin to count how many times I've heard that line from my children. For a while it seemed as if no conflict was ever settled to satisfaction as either one child or the other felt as if they got the short end of the stick. Fairness and equality aren't values only held by children, however. We all want life to be, if nothing else, fair. We want opportunities to be spread across the board. We want the punishment to be proportionate to the crime committed. Basic human rights, we believe, should be recognized regardless of who the individual is. At the end of the day, we expect our society to be fair. Nothing can spark debate like a trial in which we believe the justice system acted unfairly. Nothing can start a protest like a work environment where the salary is seen to be unfair. Nothing can raise the ire of millions like discrimination of any kind. If nothing else, we expect those around us to be fair.

So, it's a wonder that this principle of fairness and equity doesn't always extend to grace. Presented with the worst crimes imaginable, the average person will advocate for an appropriate punishment. Some will even go overboard in their zeal for justice, attempting to make an example out of the offender. Accuse the would-be judge of the same crime, however, and you get a very different response.

We are great prosecutors for others, but we are amazing

defense attorneys for ourselves. The other person should have known better. They should have been more careful. They were raised in the church. They are trying to take advantage of the system. They are playing games. They don't deserve any more chances. We shouldn't enable them. We shouldn't coddle them. We aren't teaching them any lessons. We aren't doing them any good. We have to be fair. Us, however? That's a totally different story. There were extenuating circumstances. You just don't understand. I didn't mean it. I had the best of intentions. I didn't know what I was doing. No one told me. No one was there for me. No one helped me. I just need one more chance. You're being unreasonable. I was tired. I was hungry. I was lonely. You're not being fair.

For some reason, even when we can accept grace for ourselves, we struggle to extend the same level of grace to others. The prosecution rests their case. The defense never does. We just aren't inclined to give everyone around us the same benefit of the doubt that we might give ourselves, and yet they need it. Our neighbors and colleagues and friends and family, and yes, even our enemies need the same grace we hope to apply to our lives. If we need to be forgiven, they need the same. If we need mercy, they need the same. If we need compassion, they need the same. If we need to be understood, they need the same. If we need patience, they need the same. If we could benefit from another chance, they could use the same.

Our world would be different, our political climate would be more palatable, our churches would be more compassionate, and our Christianity would be more believable if we embraced this idea of grace being extended to everyone just the same. You don't get less grace because you sin differently. It's the same. You don't get more grace because you look like me. It's the same. You don't get additional grace because you can afford it. It's the same. You don't get minimal grace because you're an opponent. It's the same. Regardless of where you're from or what you look like or what label society places on you… the grace is the same.

The grace is the same because God is the same.

He's the same God who causes the rain to fall on the deserving and the undeserving and the same God who allows the sun to shine on those who love Him and those who deny His very existence. He's the same God who provides for the poor and gives the rich the power to get wealth. He's the same God who loves all of His children, no matter where they are from, what they look like, or who they are.

Our God loves us all, forgives us all, and His grace pursues us all. I wish we would do the same.

PERSONAL REFLECTION

Why is the grace we show not always the same as the grace we receive? How can that change?

_____

_____

_____

_____

Are the people who hurt you deserving of the same grace you have been given? Why or why not?

_____

_____

_____

_____

How do we administer justice if everyone deserves the same grace? Does one exclude the other?

_____

_____

_____

_____

What am I praying about today?

_____

_____

_____

Who am I praying for today?

_____

_____

_____

PRAYER STARTER

Gracious Father, I appreciate the consistency of Your grace. My mistakes do not dilute Your grace, nor do my imperfections lessen the intensity of Your love. For this I give You praise. Help me today...

– Amen

Day 14

Something New

"I am crucified with Christ. Nevertheless, I live..."
Galatians 2:20

"Daddy, you're always trying something new!"

When they said it, they were just a tad bit exasperated. Truth be told, however, Eve and Terri are absolutely right because I am always trying something new. I'm not sure when that started, but at some point, I decided that I was tired of missing out and I wasn't going to allow fear to hold me back anymore. So, I started jumping in with both feet, so to speak, and it's been fun! Most of the time.

You see, there's always a familiar pattern when it comes to trying anything new. Before you get started there is the fear - and the fear is always there with dozens of questions and plenty of concerns. Why am I doing this? Is this safe? Am I going to be ok? What am I thinking? But, if you listen to the fear long enough, you will talk yourself out of doing just about anything! Let's face it, there's ALWAYS a good reason to say "no".

I remember my first time doing indoor rock-climbing. I'm afraid of heights and decided that the best way to conquer that fear would be to climb some 50 feet up in the air, and then use a harness to come back down. I can remember standing at the base just before my first climb, thinking, "Are you crazy?" "What are you trying to prove?" "What if you hurt yourself?" "What would everyone say?" "Why are you doing this?" "Are you sure you're not crazy?" I stood at the base and had a long conversation with myself about all the reasons why climbing that day was a bad idea. Come to think of it, I'm pretty sure that climbing that rock never actually became a "good" idea.

Getting over the fear and getting started is an important first step, but it is just that- a first step. Getting started is only the beginning. Once you get started, there's the feeling of awkwardness. This is, after all, something new, you're far from an expert and the technique isn't familiar. Your brain and body are still trying to adjust because the surroundings may be strange, the teacher is definitely different, and the language is new. This is the time when I usually second-guess myself the most. "Are you sure you want to go through with this?"

When I first started roller-skating classes (yes, there is such a thing as a roller skating class), I was one of three people at the beginners' level. My classmates were 6 and 8 years old. I'm 42. Can you picture a 42-year-old on wobbly legs trying to stay upright on roller skates and not fall over the other kids? I couldn't either, but there I was, looking and feeling incredibly awkward. The mechanics didn't come naturally, the technique was brand new, and I couldn't blend in. It was all I could not to run away and hide.

With every beginning there's going to be fear and awkwardness. With every beginning there's going to be awkwardness. That's just the way it goes. If you let those feelings control you, then you'll always confine yourself to what is comfortable, and what's comfortable may not always be what is best.

There is something new I would like for you to try.

Most people have been exposed to a religious experience that includes fear and guilt. The fear clouds our perception of God and the guilt leads us to work harder or stay away. For many, the idea of being saved by grace alone is new. And I know what it's like to try something new. First comes the fear. The fear that there will be something missing from my faith experience that will leave me lacking in my relationship with God, the fear that

I will not have sufficiently compensated God for the forgiveness of my sins, and the fear that somehow Jesus is not enough. Then there is the awkwardness. Those who surrender their will to Jesus, and trust Him for their spiritual growth and salvation know what I'm talking about. The technique of trusting in Jesus is still new, and the mechanics of not believing that God forgives you without earning it, don't come naturally. You feel wobbly and nothing feels natural.

After the awkwardness, you eventually get comfortable. That's what happens when you stick with a new thing. Eventually, the new thing isn't new anymore. You get familiar, then comfortable, and then you can share your skill with someone else. That's the life I want for you, and that's the life God wants for us all. A life where we walk with Jesus comfortably, He becomes a friend, and we develop a faith we can share with someone else. Why not try something new today?

PERSONAL REFLECTION

What was the last new thing you tried? Did it take you outside of your comfort zone? How did you deal with the fear?

_____

_____

_____

_____

How would the absence of fear or guilt make a difference in your walk with Jesus? What would that look like in your daily life?

_____

_____

_____

_____

Ephesians 2:8 calls salvation the "gift of God". What does salvation being a "gift" mean to you?
a) What do you do?   b) What do you NOT do?

_____

_____

_____

_____

What am I praying about today?

_____

_____

_____

_____

Who am I praying for today?

_____

_____

_____

_____

PRAYER STARTER

Gracious Father, I receive Your free gift of salvation and I look forward to how it will change my life. I'm excited about a walk with You that is absent of guilt and fear. I praise You for joy and peace in advance. Help me today...

_____
_____
_____
_____
_____
_____
_____
_____
_____
_____
_____
_____
_____
_____
_____
_____
_____
_____
_____
_____
_____
_____
_____
_____

– Amen

Day 15

Unstoppable

"For the gifts and calling of God are without repentance."
Romans 11:29

Niagara Falls will never fail to remind you of how small you are. See the falls in person and you won't be able to do anything but stand in amazement. Millions of gallons of water career over the falls and into the river below, completely unbothered by the onlookers and unaffected by the surroundings. Whether the temperature heats up, or drops below freezing, the waters continue to flow (although certain parts of the falls may temporarily freeze, the waters generally flow).

Regardless of your opinions about the water, it continues to flow. You may be displeased with its performance, or having a bad day, but you guessed it-the waters continue to flow. Nothing stops the water, gets in its way, or changes its course. Nothing slows it down or speeds it up, because the falls remain unaffected. They always have, they always will. Stand there long enough and you'll discover that, not only will the waters continue to flow, but there's really nothing anyone can do about it. Cross paths with the water, and you will inevitably be swept away. You can try as hard as you can to hold it back, or concentrate with all of your might, but nothing you do can make a difference. Imagine the arrogance of someone who'd think they could do such a thing. You'd be a fool to even try.

We sometimes treat God as if He is fickle. To us, He is bound by the same circumstances and held to the same limitations that confine the rest of us. Instead of a limitless God who is always in control, we prefer to think of God like He is subject to our boundaries. Maybe it makes God more manageable, or maybe it makes us more comfortable. After all, a God who can do anything is difficult to comprehend, challenging to predict, and impossible to control. Now, create a God in our own image and endow Him with our weaknesses, He's relatable. He's just like me. But what if the God I created is the furthest thing from the truth, and what if I robbed Him of His power and stole His prerogative? What if God is more than I've made Him out to be, and He is more generous than I've imagined, more loving than I ever hoped, and more powerful than I ever dreamed?

What if we served a God who could really do anything? Forgive any sin, perform any miracle, know the end from the beginning, and not be subject to any limit? That would be a God that was truly in control. His mercy would be everlasting, His plans would be permanent, and His grace would be unstoppable. He wouldn't have to change His mind.

Maybe it's time for a shift in our perspective about God. When we make promises and plans, what we are really saying is, "I will accomplish this to the best of my ability." If the situation changes and I am unable to fulfil my promise, I can't be held accountable. I have my limits after all. If I say, "I'll see you tomorrow", and I happen to be hospitalized tonight, no reasonable person would chastise me for not keeping my promise. There, marks a huge difference between us and God. When God makes a promise, He keeps it to the best of HIS ability. And His ability has no limits. This is why His grace can be sufficient and His mercy can endure forever. Your God cannot be stopped.

The sad part is, some of us actually try. We actually think that we can somehow hold God back from accomplishing His purposes for us. But just like the person standing in front of Niagara Falls, you will soon find out that you aren't that big! There's nothing you can do to make God love you more and there's nothing you can do to make God love you less. You can never be disqualified no matter who you are, and you have not crossed the point of no return no matter where you've been. My God is truly unstoppable.

I was in a car accident some years ago. As a result, the insurance company wanted to total my car. To them, the value of the car made it not worth the restoration. I didn't feel the same. It wasn't valuable to them, but the car was valuable to me. I found a master mechanic and turned the project over to him, and within days I had my car restored. Restoration didn't look likely, but it was possible because of what the master mechanic was able to do.

I would take a chance in saying that your life has a lot of mileage left, and your best is yet to come. The unstoppable grace of God can restore any "project" no matter how big. Why don't you let Him get started now?

PERSONAL REFLECTION

Have you ever been in a situation where you felt that God's grace could no longer cover you? What happened?

_____

_____

_____

_____

What are some other words for "unstoppable"? (List three below). How do those synonyms better help you understand God's grace?

_____

_____

_____

_____

Knowing that nothing can make God change His mind about you, how will you live your life differently today?

_____

_____

_____

_____

What am I praying about today?

_____

_____

_____

Who am I praying for today?

_____

_____

_____

PRAYER STARTER

Gracious Father, I praise You for Your unstoppable grace! Thank You for reminding me that nothing in this universe will ever make You change Your mind about me. Your call on my life is permanent and Your plans for me are still in effect. All I have to do is believe and obey. Help me today…

– Amen

Day 16

No Shame

"But now in Christ Jesus, you, who some time
were afar off, are made right by the blood of Christ."
Ephesians 2:13

To paraphrase the words of the apostle Paul, "Here is a trustworthy saying that deserves full acceptance"... almost every child has been embarrassed by their mom and dad.

As much as we love and cherish our parents, every kid goes through the stage where they feel they have to portray the illusion that they do, in fact, live alone. Parents? What parents? Oh, those people who dropped me off, who insist on kissing and yelling at me about not forgetting things, and who are being generally "uncool"? Those people? They just feed me, clothe me, and put a roof over my head. I promise I have no idea who they are, and I've never seen them before a day in my life!

I remember the day my mom came to my high school. I was in the 10th grade and I wasn't doing so well, so my parents thought it would be best to schedule a parent-teacher conference at the school (why did it have to be at the school?). To make matters worse, mom chose to show up around mid-morning when the students were still around. Now if she came after school, there would have been a chance that my friends wouldn't cross paths with her because they would have been gone for the day. However, at 10:30 a.m., I had to face the fact that SOMEBODY WOULD SEE HER! I was fully prepared for my life as I knew it, to end.

That morning they called my name over the intercom and asked me to come to the office. When I arrived, there she was, seated with all of my teachers in a semicircle with my academic records between them. Mom had a look on her face that communicated her displeasure with me, and as the teachers continued to share my progress, I eventually learned that the look was so well-deserved. I had not been doing well in school, but that statement didn't tell the whole story. It left out the part of the story where I had been missing homework, and goofing off in class.

Here was my mother, in front of all of these teachers, trying her best to vouch for the work ethic and diligence of her son, only to be met with evidence to the contrary. Her son wasn't working very hard at all. Indeed, the day was embarrassing, but I had no reason to be embarrassed of my mom that morning. As a concerned parent willing to make any sacrifice necessary for my success, she was holding up her end of the bargain. I wasn't applying myself, or living up to my potential. Instead of me being ashamed of my mom, she had every right to be ashamed of me.

No one likes to be embarrassed. Think about the last time you were ashamed, and you'll feel it - the anger rising from the pit of your stomach and the lump forming in the back of your throat. Of all of the emotions we experience, shame is one of the most unpleasant, and humbling. Personally, I would avoid shame at all costs, and most of us would do the same. That's why we try so hard to fit in, and why most don't draw attention to themselves intentionally. That's also why we conform to societal norms, mind our manners, and behave ourselves around polite company. After all, "Have you no shame?" Yet while we have no reason to be ashamed of our Heavenly Father, He has every reason to be ashamed of us.

Think about it. We serve a perfect God who gives us many blessings and has promised to withhold no good thing. He will supply every need, and He protects from danger. His love is unconditional, and He answers our prayers. God holds up His end of the bargain. It's the other end that can honestly be called into question. The other end, our end, is full of failure, regret and downright shame. It's not that we should be embarrassed by God, but God should be embarrassed by us.

And if He was embarrassed I couldn't blame Him. My constant excuses about "being human" and "not being perfect", wouldn't cut it for me either. Even I get tired of seeing myself fail, or get sick of seeing myself come up short. He is a Holy God, a perfect Father, and Creator of heaven and earth. The sovereign King of the universe. He is Alpha and Omega. And you and I with our bad habits and bad decisions are the best He can muster? I'd be ashamed of me too.

Except, Hebrews 2:11 says that Jesus, "is not ashamed to call us brothers". Can you believe it? Even though we are who we are, He claims us as His own! We are related to Jesus, and He's proud of it. Our Heavenly Father would not only take us to school, but He would walk with us right into our classroom and sit down beside us for the entire student population to see. All the while holding our hand because He is not ashamed! We might act shamefully, but He claims us anyhow. He has no problem letting the entire world know that you are His child.

You may look at your life and think you don't have much of which you can be proud, but God does not feel the same way. He's proud of you! He claims you! You belong to Him and He doesn't mind letting the universe know. He is not ashamed, and come to think of it, I'll walk with my head held high too.

PERSONAL REFLECTION

When was the last time you've been embarrassed? How did you handle it? How did it make you feel?

_____

_____

_____

_____

When was the last time you felt ashamed when talking to God? Did you open up to Him anyway?

_____

_____

_____

_____

List three people who are proud of you. How does having their support make you feel? How does God "not being ashamed" of you make you feel? Are you proud of Him?

_____

_____

_____

What are you praying for today?

_____

_____

_____

_____

Who am I praying for today?

_____

_____

_____

_____

PRAYER STARTER

Gracious Father, You are not ashamed of me even though at times I have been ashamed of my behavior. Thank You for never giving up on me. Help me today...

_____

_____

_____

_____

_____

_____

_____

_____

_____

_____

_____

_____

_____

_____

_____

_____

_____

_____

_____

_____

_____

_____

– Amen

Day 17

Ask Him

"Ask, and it shall be given you; seek, and ye shall find;
knock, and it shall be opened unto you:"
Matthew 7:7

I'll never forget the night I almost met my childhood hero.

Mom had taken my brother and I to the Dorton arena one night to see professional wrestling. This wasn't just any event, however, because on the card that night was the one and only "Nature Boy" Rick Flair. I could hardly contain myself as we made our way down the narrow aisles in the darkened arena and waited for our show to start. As I looked around the arena, staff and performers getting ready for the show. My eyes scanned the back of the arena and all of a sudden, there he was! Standing with a group against a wall just a few feet away was the man we all came to see. I couldn't believe my eyes! There he was, in the flesh, the "Nature Boy." I can remember it like it was yesterday. Him looking larger than life, my heart beating faster than ever, and time crawling as everything ground to a halt. And then there was my mother's voice…

"Why don't you ask him?"

Mom knew I wanted Rick Flair's autograph. Scratch that, mom knew I NEEDED Rick Flair's autograph. If years of seeing me hold the television hostage on Saturday nights so that I could watch wrestling had told her nothing else, they told her that I needed Rick Flair's autograph. Now here he was, just 30 feet away. Just 30 feet and one request between me and the meeting of a lifetime. Just 30 feet and one request away from a totally life-altering encounter that would create a lasting memory. Just 30 feet and one request, and yet I couldn't do it. I was way too shy, and 30 feet was way too far. He was way too big, and the security guards were way too intimidating. So, I muttered some excuse about not wanting to bother him and shoved the dreams of meeting my hero back down into my gut. I would miss the opportunity of a lifetime, because I couldn't bring myself to ask.

For some of you, boldness isn't a problem. For some, asking is easy. For those of us who are introverted and shy, however, the approach can be a mountain too difficult to climb. We can't "just ask". There are way too many "What if's" to think about. "Just ask", seems simple enough until you factor in all the things that can go wrong. I could ask and be embarrassed, or I could ask and be turned away. I could ask, and my request be out of place or out of turn. Asking can be serious, risky business. Better to not be embarrassed or rejected. Better to do without than to suffer wounded pride. Better to not ask at all.

But there are some things we cannot do without, like grace. Grace is a universal necessity - no one functions without it and no one survives apart from it. We all need it, and we all want it, because who doesn't want grace! Who doesn't want to be forgiven their past mistakes and gifted the clean slate of a second chance? Who doesn't want to see a new day, begin a new chapter, and start a new life! Maybe this might be too dramatic for you, but every new year's resolution ever made tells me the same thing - most people wouldn't mind hitting the reset button if they could. The problem is, we are under the impression that we can't. Our shortcomings are too much, and our Savior seems too scary. Sure, He's there. Available and able. But is it really that simple? Can I go to Him again? What about the last time? Won't God think I'm a hypocrite? My life is complicated and I'm a repeat offender. So are you sure it's really that simple?

I'm here to tell you that it is. If you want God's forgiveness, if you need His mercy, if you want His grace, all you have to do is ask! God is not in the business of holding on to our faults nor is He in the habit of holding out on grace. He bestows it freely, gives it liberally, administers it generously and shares it indiscriminately. There's no form to fill out, no process through which you have to go, and no payment to be made. All you have to do is ask.

Years ago, I purchased my first home. What surprised me about the purchase was the amount of paperwork it took to get a loan. The bank wanted my entire life story - in detail, with no gaps. I can understand the thoroughness, because banks aren't just giving money away, and money doesn't grow on trees. Grace, however does come from a Savior who hung upon a tree, and Jesus IS giving it away. To everyone. Even me. Even you.

All you have to do is ask.

PERSONAL REFLECTION

Are you comfortable asking for help? Why? Why not?

_____

_____

_____

_____

Consider Jacob's wrestling match in Genesis 32. Verse 28 says "I will not let you go until you bless me..." Describe Jacob's cry for help. Have you ever approached God that way?

_____

_____

_____

_____

Grace is available to everyone. What is one thing you can do today to share that message with someone?

_____

_____

_____

_____

What are you praying about today?

_____

_____

_____

_____

Who are you praying for today?

_____

_____

_____

_____

PRAYER STARTER

Gracious Father, I'm grateful for the fact that You NEVER get tired of me asking for Your grace! Thank You for Your patience and generosity towards me. I am always in need, but You are always available to supply. Lord, I appreciate You. Help me today....

– Amen

Day 18

Don't Miss It

"Search the Scriptures, for in them ye think ye have eternal life: and they are they which testify of me."
John 5:39

"The heights of great men reached and kept
Were not attained by sudden flight
But they while their companions slept
Were toiling upward in the night."
– Henry Wadsworth Longfellow

Dr. Iola Brown would be proud. I'm pretty sure she doesn't remember this, but my elementary school principal, Dr. Brown, drilled this poem into our heads. She took every opportunity to remind us that we were there to study, and study hard. If we applied ourselves, there would be no limit to the heights of accomplishment we would achieve. Study and it would be at your fingertips. Be diligent and success would be your sweet reward. I'm sure Dr. Brown taught us many poems and left us with many sayings, but this verse as well as its underlying meaning, stayed with me long after I left the walls of Unique Christian Academy. If I learned nothing else at "UCA", I learned to study hard.

I can't honestly say that I maintained the same love for study throughout the remainder of my academic career (unfortunately, I also discovered "fun" and that was all she wrote). However, I admire those who study – especially the word of God. The Bible says, "Study to show thyself approved…" which seems to suggest that the Bible has a bit more than first encounters for us at the surface. We are invited to dig, and encouraged to explore. Go deeper, think harder, stay longer, and look again.

"Study to show thyself approved". (Side note: I wonder how many misunderstandings could be resolved if we wouldn't just read but "study"? I wonder how many doctrinal "disagreements"- read "arguments", would be resolved if we would take the time to go beneath what the words on the page seem to say and actually take the time to study... but I digress).

We are encouraged to study, and I for one commend the scholars who actually do. The problem, however, comes when the results of your study lead away from the only conclusion that matters. "Search the scriptures, for in them ye think ye find eternal life. And these are they which testify of ME". In all your study, you should find Jesus. Beneath the surface of the scriptures, you should encounter Jesus. While pondering the profundity of any given passage, you should not help but come across Jesus. The entire Bible is the story of Jesus and His plan to bring the human race back to Him. If you miss everything, you can't miss Jesus. If you find nothing else, you must find Jesus. "These are they which testify of me."

My heart breaks for those who don't see the beauty of the Son of God who gave His life for them. With all the grace packed into every word of the Bible, somehow, they missed it! We've all met those people, and some of us, are those people. The love of Jesus seems obvious from the first page of Genesis to the last page of Revelation. He created us, pursues us, and wants to be with us. He died for us, and is coming back for us. It's all right there! "These are they which testify of me..."

I'm becoming hilariously forgetful. Not the kind of forgetful that causes you to misplace your glasses or lose your car keys. It's more like the kind of forgetful that makes you look for your glasses while they are still on your head or search for your car keys with the engine running. That kind of forgetful. I'm learning again and again that it's even possible to miss the obvious if you're not careful. You can spend all afternoon looking for the remote control you just happened to be sitting on. You can walk around in circles looking for a cell phone that's been charging the entire time. If you're not careful, you can miss the obvious even though it's as plain as the nose on your face.

How's your relationship with Jesus? If you've found yourself hesitant to come back to Him after your last mistake, be careful. If you find yourself talking to Him less and chiding yourself more, be careful. Even as a Christian, you might just be missing the obvious. You might be missing a truth that's as plain as the nose on your face. Jesus came to save, and His heart is full of compassion and love. If you don't see that as you study the Bible, keep looking. If you don't embrace that as a part of your relationship with Christ, keep looking.

His grace is a truth that you can't afford to miss.

PERSONAL REFLECTION

How is it possible to study the Bible and miss the love of Jesus? Have you ever missed Jesus in your study?

_____

_____

_____

What are some of the reasons why discovering Jesus would not be top priority when studying the Word? How can you challenge and change those reasons in your life?

_____

_____

_____

_____

Describe what a religious experience that doesn't make understanding Jesus the top priority looks like to you. How can you avoid this pitfall?

_____

_____

_____

_____

What am I praying for today?

_____

_____

_____

Who am I praying about today?

_____

_____

_____

_____

PRAYER STARTER

Gracious Father, I thank You for Jesus, the center of my joy. I thank You for the impact He has made in my life and I thank You for the Bible that reveals His will for me. Help me today…

– Amen

Day 19

The Shortcut

*"Come unto me all ye that labor and are heavy laden
and I will give you rest."*
Matthew 11:28

Walking home with my father after school was always an adventure. For starters, he walked fast (at least it was fast for my 8-year-old legs). As we traveled down Flatbush avenue, my nose assaulted by the smell of pizza that seemed to come around every corner... it was all I could do to keep up as he pulled me along the way, keeping me away from the confusion of the city streets and making me stay close to him. The most interesting (and by that, I mean "terrifying") part of the walk home always came about two blocks from our apartment when dad decided to take a shortcut. There was an alley that took us more directly from Flatbush avenue to our home, and dad thought it was a good idea to save a few steps by taking the shortcut. In theory, this was a good idea. Any reasonable person could concede that this shortcut could be helpful, and therefore, useful. After all, why do anything the hard way when you can do it the easy way? Why go the long way when you can cut some distance off of your trip? The shortcut made sense, but I was an eight-year-old boy who didn't feel like being sensible. Short as it was, I was terrified of the alley, I would much rather walk the long way home. Take me through the process. Subject me to the extra steps. Make the trip harder. I don't care! So long as I don't have to go that way.

What was it about the long way that appealed to me so much? Maybe it's the same thing about the "long way" that appeals to us all. It feels more normal. Even if it is harder, longer, and more tiring, the long way feels like the way things are supposed to be. Think about it. Jesus invites us to Him while in the midst of our confusion and strife, but that just doesn't feel right. It feels like a shortcut- a dark alley down which we just don't feel comfortable going. I'll stay away instead, waiting for the moment when I've earned the privilege of a relationship with God again. Working hard to make myself worthy, or at least a little cleaner, humbler, or more sincere. More mature, more sure, or better. Step by step, inch by inch, we take the long way because that's the way we think things should be.

The long way meshes with our value system. You see, there's something about the grind about which we can be proud. Hard work, dedication, an iron will, and a strong back. Long hours, short nights, no vacations and no excuses. I busted my hump for what I wanted, and it got me where I am today - and for that I can be proud. I didn't take any handouts, breaks, or shortcuts. I welcomed the challenge, and did it the hard way. I ate lightning and produced thunder. I didn't shy away from the pain, but rose to the occasion and met the challenge. See how good that feels? Even as I was writing it my chest puffed out just a little bit, my head picked up, and I even felt a little taller (which is great for me because I'm really not that tall) There's something about the long way that reinforces the pride within. While the shortcut does just that, it cuts. It cuts my pride and it cuts out the credit I can take. It cuts the reward I think I deserve, and it cuts out self - me. The shortcut to Jesus cuts me all the way out.

"Come unto me..." That's the shortcut to Jesus. Notice how straightforward, uncomplicated and direct it is? "Come unto me". It's the most no-frills approach one could ever imagine. No qualifies, prerequisites, or preliminaries. Just come. No process, preparation, or pretense. Just come. No time limits, deadlines, or excuses needed. Just come. "Come unto me". It is as simple, and yet as unsafe a command as could possibly be given. You see, this isn't the long way. There's no victory we can claim, no strength to which we can point, and no process we can boast about mastering. There is only grace. There is only Jesus. There is only the invitation. There is only – "Come".

"Come unto me". It cuts out all of our pride and only leaves Jesus. It saves us the steps of our self-sufficiency and only leaves Jesus. It negates what we know, and how long we've known it, how well we've done it and who else has seen it. It also negates all that other stuff that didn't matter then, doesn't matter now, and will never matter in the future. It leaves (you guessed it), just Jesus. That's the short cut I'm afraid of, but it's the shortcut I need. You see, I'm tired of walking. Aren't you? Life's journey will leave you exhausted if you aren't careful. There's a lot of road ahead and it's hard to keep up. I don't know about you but I'm tired of the ups and downs. Tired of worrying and doubting. Tired of the tears. Just tired - I could use the rest.

Jesus says "Come unto me…" That's all. Nothing else. Just come. Leave your burdens, and stop trying to earn it, figure it out, walking so far, and trying so hard! Come! Take the shortcut!

You'll have a much better time getting home.

PERSONAL REFLECTION

When do you feel most comfortable coming to Jesus? Is there ever a time when you do not feel comfortable praying or communing with Him?

_____

_____

_____

_____

Is there ever an inappropriate time to pray? Why? Why not? How does your answer currently affect your prayer life?

_____

_____

_____

_____

"And I will give you rest". Describe below what the idea of "rest" means to you:

_____

_____

_____

_____

What are you praying about today?

_____

_____

_____

_____

Who are you praying for today?

_____

_____

_____

_____

PRAYER STARTER

Gracious Father, You have extended the invitation for me to "Come" and I am responding. I am weak and heavy-laden and right now, I bring my burdens to You. Help me today...

_____

_____

_____

_____

_____

_____

_____

_____

_____

_____

_____

_____

_____

_____

_____

_____

_____

_____

_____

_____

_____

_____

– Amen

Day 20

Grace to Guide

"He leads me in the paths of righteousness
for His name's sake."
Psalm 23:3

If you're going to travel, you'd better learn how to follow directions. I've learned that one the hard way. Over and over again.

I've lost track of how many times I've gotten lost. The cities and circumstances vary, but the story is usually the same. With a guidance system staring me in the face I set out on my journey. I'm fairly confident because after all, I know where I'm going. The GPS is programmed, there's gas in the car, and I have lots of experience traveling along roads just like this one. There's no way I cannot reach my destination. And so, I set out with all the promise of a fruitful journey. The directions seem simple, the routine gets boring, the road looks lonely, and I get distracted. At some point it happens, not every time, but often enough. At some point I get distracted, and I get lost. The GPS is programmed, there's gas in the car, and I have lots of experience traveling along roads just like this one. And yet I am lost, because I did not follow directions.

Getting from one place to another seems so simple. So why aren't we better at it? It's really not that hard! We should be able to make progress and yet, that's not always the case. Especially when traveling down this particularly difficult and windy road called "life". Every trip starts out the same. We know where we want to go, and we have experience traveling. And yet, every person who has found themselves lost at any point in life will confess, if they ware honest with you (and with themselves for that matter), that they started getting lost the minute they stopped following the directions.

Look at God's Word and you'll see them- the directions. They seem so simple. Everything is clear and straightforward (although we have a tendency to complicate and muddle it). "The law of the Lord is perfect, converting the soul. The testimony of the Lord is sure, making wise the simple." And speaking of simple, that's exactly what God's directions are. They may be difficult to accept, but they aren't difficult to understand. In fact, they're just the opposite. No layers, very little nuance, and no complications. It's all so simple. So simple, in fact, that the routine gets boring, the road looks lonely, and we get distracted. And we get lost.

Being lost can be frustrating and upsetting. (I mean, who wouldn't be upset after missing that obvious exit!) Get lost with a back-seat driver and you'll be driven to the point of madness. They may not say it, but the suggestion that "This looks familiar" and "I've seen that sign before" will remind you that we're lost and it's ALL YOUR FAULT! (By the way, if you are that co-pilot allow me to assure you that you are NOT HELPING! Just FYI…)

But as upset as I am, the truth remains - I didn't follow the directions. Neither did you. We did our own thing, went our own way, got distracted, and missed the turn. Driving faster won't fix it, and neither will yelling at the other passengers. Turning up the music might drown out the internal alarms that remind you that you're going in the wrong direction, but none of the above will fix it. We're lost, and we didn't follow the directions.

I said none of the above would fix the situation, but I never said the situation couldn't be fixed.

The same guidance system I tend to ignore knows just how to deal with people like me. Sometimes it will simply remind me that I've taken a wrong turn (with just a hint of an attitude that I don't appreciate) and attempt to convince me to turn around. Other times, when I make a wrong turn the GPS will do something called "recalculating". It will take into account the fact that I didn't follow the directions, and it will give me opportunities to get back on track. No matter how lost I get, the guidance system will either recalculate or remind me of the original plan.

What it never does is leave me alone.

God's instructions are there to be followed, and should be followed. But what if you haven't followed them? What if you haven't followed directions? What if you have made mistakes? What if you have gone your own way? Sometimes God will recalculate and give you the opportunity to get to where you are supposed to go without retracing your steps and reliving the pain of your past. Other times God will remind you of the original plan, and like Jonah, you will have to go to Nineveh. There's just no way around it. Either way, the good news is that the guidance system never stops working. It never shuts down or leaves you by yourself to figure it out. You are never left alone. You didn't follow the instructions then, but you have another opportunity to follow God's instructions now. One mistake doesn't have to lead to another, and one problem doesn't have to be compounded by another. There's plenty of road left on this journey, and the guidance system still works. God hasn't given up on you. He still intends to get you home.

PERSONAL REFLECTION

Has distraction ever caused you to stray from God's will for your life? How did you recognize that you were distracted? Have you gotten back on track?

_____

_____

_____

_____

List three things that keep us from following God's instructions. How can you remove those obstacles from your life?

_____

_____

_____

Have you received a second chance to follow God's instructions? What steps are you taking to ensure that you don't repeat the same mistakes?

_____

_____

_____

_____

What are you praying about today?

_____

_____

_____

_____

Who are you praying for today?

_____

_____

_____

_____

PRAYER STARTER

Gracious Father, Time and time again I get distracted and refuse to follow Your clear instructions. I thank You that You are always patient with me when I stray, and You welcome me with open arms when I return. I want to develop the habit of consistently following You. Help me today...

– Amen

Day 21

From Where You Are

"And when he came to himself, he said, How many hired servants of my father's have bread enough and to spare, and I perish with hunger!"
Luke 15:17

Staring at a subway map in Paris, a cell phone in my hand, and confusion sprawled across my face, I squinted and struggled to find information that would tell me where I was, so I could figure out where I wanted to go. I soon found the "ideal point" (the arrow that designates where one is on the map in case you were wondering) but knowing my location didn't change my situation. It only led to disappointment as it provided confirmation that I was not where I wanted to be.

For each of us, life's "locator" tells a story. For most, the drama is enough to shake even the most stubborn faith. So many are not where they want to be. Langston Hughes once asked a question, "What happens to a dream deferred?" I never quite figured out what happens to the dream, but I can tell you what happens to the dreamers. I see them all the time. Their eyes are filled with regret, and their shoulders sag as the untapped potential weighs them down. Their steps are just a tad slow from being tired of taking so many of life's wrong turns, and eyebrows furrowed as they considered what might have been. I don't know what happens to a dream deferred, but I can tell you what happens to the dreamers. They end up disappointed. They end up with regrets. They ended up questions.

For the "Ex-dreamer", there are so many questions: "How did

I get here?", "Whose fault is this?", "How do I fix it?", and "Is it too late?" For them, recognizing where they just isn't enough. Confirmation that they aren't where they are supposed to be isn't going to cut it. The ideal point is just an indicator that they've missed the mark and a reminder that they've veered away from the original plan.

I know where I am. Where can I go from here?

One look at God's plan for my life and I get excited. What an amazing plan God has for me! What an incredible God I serve! Another look at God's plan for my life and I sink into despair. Look at how much time I've wasted. Think of what might have been! Regret is the boyfriend you need to break up with, but he's still around because you have history. You're tired of people's questions, not getting any younger, and afraid of starting over. Truth is, starting over is exactly what God wants you and I to do.

The past can never be changed, and every decision made becomes a matter of permanent record. Like it or not, you are where you are, and it is what it is. You should be finished with it, but the problem with the past is that while you may be finished with it, the devil is not finished with you! He will constantly remind you not only of where you've been but of where you are. He will remind you that it was your bad decisions that got you to this point, and remind you that it is your fault that you've missed opportunities. He will remind you of how successful you could have been, how far you could have gone, and how much you could have had, if you had only... And then he'll tell you that you can't leave. You can't move on. You can't go back. You can't go anywhere. You and your past have "history", and you're not getting any younger, and you're in no position to start over - even if this isn't where you want to be.

Here's the good news: If where you are, isn't where you want to be, you can start walking NOW! When the prodigal son came to his senses, he didn't have to ask permission or do anything special. He just got up and left from right where he was, so don't let anyone tell you that you can't do the same. Have you passed your exit? Sure? Grace says you can always turn around. Have you missed your shot? Maybe! Grace says you can always try again. Has the time passed? It always does. The clock is still running but thank God it hasn't run out. Have you squandered your second chance? Probably, but grace provides another chance, and you can take the opportunity to start over. You can go back. You can try again. You can be restored. You can make it - from right where you are.

PERSONAL REFLECTION

Is your life where you want it to be? (career, relationships, finances, spiritual life, etc.) If not, what's stopping you from getting there?

_____

_____

_____

_____

If you were forced to go back to age 16 and live your life over again, list three things you would do differently:

_____

_____

_____

_____

While we cannot erase our past, we can create a new future with Jesus. How can today be the first day of the rest of your life?

_____

_____

_____

_____

What are you praying about today?

_____

_____

_____

_____

Who are you praying for today?

_____

_____

_____

_____

PRAYER STARTER

Gracious Father, I am grateful that I don't have to run from my past in order to enjoy a future with You. I thank You for redeeming me and giving me the privilege of a new life with You. Help me today...

_____

_____

_____

_____

_____

_____

_____

_____

_____

_____

_____

_____

_____

_____

_____

_____

_____

_____

_____

_____

_____

_____

– Amen

ABOUT THE AUTHOR

Gamal Alexander is a passionate storyteller whose mission is to help others to communicate more effectively while himself telling the story of Jesus' love. Born in Brooklyn, New York and raised in Raleigh, North Carolina, he now lives in Southern California where he pastors the Compton Community Church. He coaches, speaks, and writes regularly while traveling across the country. He is the father of two daughters, Faith and Grace. You can find out more about Gamal by visiting www.gamalalexander.com.

CPSIA information can be obtained
at www.ICGtesting.com
Printed in the USA
FSHW020336300619

9 781948 877176